POETRY now

OCCASIONAL LAUGHTER

Edited by

Heidi Latronico

First published in Great Britain in 1999 by
POETRY NOW
Remus House,
Coltsfoot Drive,
Woodston,
Peterborough, PE2 9JX
Telephone (01733) 898101
Fax (01733) 313524

All Rights Reserved

Copyright Contributors 1999

HB ISBN 0 75430 717 4
SB ISBN 0 75430 718 2

FOREWORD

Although we are a nation of poets we are accused of not reading poetry, or buying poetry books. After many years of listening to the incessant gripes of poetry publishers, I can only assume that the books they publish, in general, are books that most people do not want to read.

Poetry should not be obscure, introverted, and as cryptic as a crossword puzzle: it is the poet's duty to reach out and embrace the world.

The world owes the poet nothing and we should not be expected to dig and delve into a rambling discourse searching for some inner meaning.

The reason we write poetry (and almost all of us do) is because we want to communicate: an ideal; an idea; or a specific feeling. Poetry is as essential in communication, as a letter; a radio; a telephone, and the main criteria for selecting the poems in this anthology is very simple: they communicate.

CONTENTS

Stuck	Caroline J Sammout	1
School for Fools	Paula John	2
Singles Bars And Sixties Stars	Jean Mary Wright	3
Laughter - Past, Present And Future	John Hooley	4
Darn It!	Joan E Blisset	5
Sunday Afternoon	Joan Beedle	6
From This Moment On	Travis Applegate	8
A Poem To Ponder	Rachel Taylor	10
Do You Believe That The World Will End?	Antonio Martorelli	11
The Haymakers	Margaret Parry	12
Strawberry Fields Revisited	Ian Barton	13
A Child's Memory	Christine Slurey	14
Vers Le Soir	Lorcan O'Connor	15
Letting Go	Heather Kirkpatrick	16
Candlewick Sweetheart	Rob Herd	17
Just For Tonight	William Price	18
Death On The Beach	Barbara King	19
Survival	Charles Butler	20
Private Health Care Plan	Don Goodwin	22
Sandstone Afternoon	Paul Andrew Jones	23
Enigma: CLIV (b)-?	J Duncan Warmingham	24
Sue	Steve Harris	25
Circle Of Life	Deborah Morris	26
Sad Pad	John L Wright	27
You	Victoria Joan Theedam	28
I'm The Man	Saheda Khan	29
The Reluctant Visitor	T M Wright	30
A Man And His Willie	Rachael Hewett	31
Phobias	Jean Rendell	32
A Woman's World	T B Smith	33
The Jacket	W Fred Tabaczynski	34
The Birthday Cake	Kathy French	35
Wesley The Wasp	Dohmnall Le Gai	36
Druids Harbour	Brian Haswell	37

HMP	Jonathon Covington	38
My Wife	Denys George Hill	39
The Old Wooden Shed	Sandra Brisck	40
Looking For A Path	M Rossi	41
Wrongful Attraction	Laura McAulay	42
Millennium	J Brohee	43
The Book	R Davidson	44
The Race	Edna Hunt	45
Farewell Rabin	James Peter King Appiah	46
Blue Eyes	Richard Higgins	47
The Legend Of Jerai-Shul	Dana Adler	48
When The Daffodils Bloom	Stan Davenport	50
A Meal Of An Ode	Lesley Tomlinson	51
There Is A Wonderful Beginning	Jackie Gaish	52
Life	Louise Gough	53
Sweet Dreams	Ann Beard	54
Ghosts	Jean Paisley	55
World Without End?	Patricia J Harding	56
I Surrender	Kenneth Mood	58
Bradford's Complexion	Benny Howell	59
My Rabbit	Tina Eccles	60
The Modern Executioner	Lachlan Taylor	61
How Can We Tell?	Bill Hayles	62
Albatross	Rodger Moir	63
Flower Girl	Alan Jones	64
The Awards	B Page	65
When I Was Young	P Edwards	66
Secret Love	Polina Belle McCann	67
Corner Shop	Adrian Vale	68
Gypsy Bride	Stephanie Reynolds	70
The Choice	David Hazlet	71
Feeling Hungry	Claire Louise Carter	72
Morning Thoughts	William Price	73
The Hand Of Destiny	Jarzie	74
The Gift	Tom Ritchie	75
A Purple Ocean	Craig Shuttleworth	76
April Showers	Philip Trivett	77
A Hat Stand-Off	P Grubb	78

The Complete Fool	A Wilkinson	79
An April Fool	Colin Allsop	80
April In Uppermill	Betty Lightfoot	81
By Word Of Mouth	Frances Cox	82
An April Shower	Bob Hessey	83
April Fool's Dad	Darshan Marawha	84
Gavin Butterworth's Coming To Tea	Marilyn M Fowler	85
April 1st	Claire Farragher	86
April Fool	Phyllis M Dunn	88
April Fool	C Halliburton	89
The Know-All	Marguerite Porthouse	90
Hair (A Personal Reflection)	Peter Bauer	91
Lara's Law	Jackie Durnin	92
Heartsob	N C Bain	93
Anno Domini	A O Jones	94
Joy Of Friendship	P Patel	95
Laughter - The Best Medicine	Kathleen Willis	96
The Elephant	Jean Oxley	97
Our Baby Liam	Lee Round	98
Haiku Musings At The Zoo	Albert Russo	99
Raise The Tone	Ann Weavers	100
Laughter	Norah M Bennett	101
Transformation	N A Milne	102
Life Grows Like That	Debra Neale	103
Laughter	John G Horley	104
Gene Crazy	Bert Booley	105
Shirley's 50th	Carol Somerfield	106
The Hospital Visit	Dawn Shaw	107
The Divine Chuckle	Margaret Holmes	108
Teething Troubles	J Greenacre	109
Fishing In The Street	Paul Wadge	110
Smile	Sheila M Gannon	111
Laughing At You	Keith L Powell	112
The Haircut	Gordon Bannister	113
Catalyst!	Di Bagshawe	114
Little Green-Eyed God	Monica F James	115
Red Ridin' Rap	Norm Whittle	116

Diamond Wedding	R Gaveston-Knight	118
Girds	Janet Brown	119
The Appointment Card	Shaun Gilberton	120
Laughter, The Best Medicine	Barbara Gates	121
The Too-Big-Yin	Bob Mackay	122
Lo, The Poor Farmer	Norman Chandler	123
Pavonia	Paul Cozens	124
The Last Laugh	Margaret Thorpe	125
The Charmed Life Of Finny The Fish	Trevor Vincent	126

STUCK
(Dedicated to Sue)

Panic starts to set the tone, she's prowling now inside,
The carriage it's so empty, she's trying not to cry.
'Help, I don't know what to do, I'm all alone in here!'
She stares into the darkness and fills herself with fear.
The track below is all there is, no platform to alight.
She's alone here in the siding, I hear her comic plight.
The driver he's gone AWOL, his shift came to an end.
But whilst chatting on her mobile, his train she did ascend.
Departure came before its time, she thought this was quite strange,
A train with just one passenger leaves early for a change?
But the journey ended quickly, it wasn't homeward bound,
Just resting for the evening away from sight and sound.
Frantic now she's dialling upon that phone of hers,
'I'm stuck, can someone help me?' She yells her high-pitched words.
Suddenly out of the gloom she sees her train arrive.
Open-mouthed she watches as it leaves her far behind.
A hat, she spies out on the track, bopping to and fro.
She dives and then begins to pound upon the flank window.
Waving hands and slamming fists, the guard cannot ignore,
His gaze is fixed in disbelief as she motions to the door.
At last the train is moving up to the platform's side,
Composed but somewhat red-faced, she thanks him for the ride.
'Did you not see the driver? Left, half hour ago, alone.'
'No,' she says defeated . . .' I was on my mobile phone!'

Caroline J Sammout

SCHOOL FOR FOOLS

We had to think of something quick
The date was drawing near
We needed to confuse them all
It was our final year

The teachers knew most of the pranks
That pupils often pulled
So we needed something special
For the coming *April Fools*

We finally came up with it
This idea was profound
We'll get them in an uproar
Cause we'll change the classes round

On *April Fools*, we started
The 5th years made their move
We took ourselves from one class
To totally different rooms

The teachers took a long time
To try and work it out
When reading from the register
No pupils called out loud

They headed to the office
In case they had it wrong
And double-checked the rota
For the classes they had on

It suddenly occurred to them
The clever thing we'd done
By then though it was too late
As the final bell had rung

Paula John

SINGLES BARS AND SIXTIES STARS

There are those who may declare, this old bird's way past her prime,
And that she should behave sedately, when having a good time.
But . . . feeling somewhat dreary - divorce no cause for fun -
My outlook needed brightening, 'cause my attitude's still young!
So I tried a singles bar: found it *not* my cup of tea -
I grabbed me bag and dashed back home, to digital TV -
(I prefer romantic movies, to furtive glances in bars!)
Then I went to see a show, which featured *Sixties Stars*!
Where I worshipped past pop heroes - got magic autographs -
From the distance of the dance-floor: nostalgic tunes . . . and laughs!

Already top musicians, with feel-good humour they impressed us;
Gerry, Peter, Freddie, Wayne; still cream of Homo Northwestus.
Marsden's famous firm philosophy? 'Make your audience feel fine!'
Laced with wacky anecdotes, his set uplifts like vintage wine.
No Milk Today for Herman - or that amiable showman, *Noone* -
Of infectious cheeky grin; 'cos *Sunshine Girl*, he's leaving soon!
At risqué cracks from *Garrity* - whose short-shorts keep us *Dreaming* -
We embarrassingly titter . . . no more inclined for screaming.
If in jest *Fontana* proffers slurs, that *some* consider shocking,
Follicly challenged, he doffs his hat! - *this* gesture, is *self*-mocking!

Their comedy's augmented, with *Bo Diddley* beats, and vocals,
So I flex protesting limbs, as I squint through new bifocals.
Middle-aged I may well be (or in the process of growing),
But who cares if the wrinkles, are more evidently showing?
I no longer kid myself - I know I can't remove them -
(But that nice man at the chemist, sells a cream that *might*
                                        improve them!)
Teen-girl happy memories linger; I can forget the ageing years,
As I twirl, and snap me fingers, the beat pulsating round me ears.
So *Hang On* to that Zimmer frame *Sloopy*, and the creaky rocking chair;
Clear the floor for this cheery old groupie, with the bleached
                                        blonde hair!

Jean Mary Wright

Laughter - Past, Present And Future

Think back away from Dismal Thoughts, think back to times long past
Think of all those Circus Clowns at whom we laughed for so long
we thought it would forever last

Also remember when we came away from such a happy scene
That we could if we cared to, remember that Happiness where we had been

But we have moved on and ahead and the years and life
have taken their toll
and we must take firm and solid steps
to climb up and out from this dismal hole

The answer lies in looking ahead and seeing the best in life
Let laughter walk with us each day whether we are man or wife

Laughter will erase all strife
as once Laughter reappears out goes Pain in Life

It is never easy if we are low or down and feeling sad and glum
to try to stand up and pretend that all is fine and dandy
when in reality life had made us numb

And although it's hard we must try to bring the Sunshine swiftly through
so when in the morning or the night you look into the mirror and see the view
the healing starts in that mirror when you must laugh at you

Then in the street you smile and smile and you will feel like new
for as you smile for others the Sunshine will shine for you

John Hooley

DARN IT!

Darn it! I left the fire on,
Darn it! I'll do it again.
It's easily done. It costs a bomb!
You think you've thought
And then you think again.
It's no use. However much you try to be
Perfect, it's an impossibility.
So careful. Must get the bills down!
Switch everything off when I go out,
Check it all. Check it again.
Answer that call! Telephone's ringing.
A little chat, well that's that.
There's the doorbell! Answer it now!
Don't dilly-dally! Someone's waiting!
They've arrived! 'Are you ready?
Come on now! We must go!
Time's getting on! Can't be late!
Just remember we made a date!'
'OK! I'm coming! Everything's off! Let's go!'
'Enjoy the day?' 'Of course I did
It's what we planned, so there you go!'
Arriving home, unlock the door . . .
And you were so very sure
You'd switched everything off.
Blazing away! 'Darn it!
The fire's on! It'll cost a bomb!'

Joan E Blisset

SUNDAY AFTERNOON
(Lone Raider - London 1940)

As a child it came,
one Sunday afternoon;
interfering through the quiet
after-dinner snooze.

Throbbing, jerking engine,
limping through the air.
Mother, Father puzzled -
sensed approaching fear!

Wings hovered, dark, menacing -
signs appeared -
black emblems, swastikas,
marked here and there!

To life it came,
spitting through the air -
red agonising fire,
dipped, rose,
twisted, turned -
to catch us in its stare.

All hell let loose,
glass shattered.
As one we turned, clattered
down the cellar stairs.
Dark engulfed us there.
Walls moved in and earth
trembled in the air!

Left to its own devices,
the metal did its worst;
thundering, deafening,
heat, sparks, shrapnel,
dust rose, accursed.

Roof, chimney, windows,
dissolved helplessly,
crumbled beneath the force
that roared tremendously,
until all settled -
defeated - silent - wearily.

Silence quite unknown,
inexperienced,
as we appeared into a
white shrouded world,
broken only by spades
digging, chinking, useless aids.

Human form took place
their hopeless task -
to extract life from the void tombs.
we lived
we breathed -
that Sunday afternoon.

Joan Beedle

FROM THIS MOMENT ON
*(Dedicated to my loving wife Delline
who has inspired me)*

From the first day I laid eyes on you.
I knew you were the one.
The one for me and I for you.
From the first day you touched my heart with love.
I made a vow.

To Love.
To Trust.
To Respect.
To be Loyal unto you.
To be honest with you.
As you are unto me.

From this moment.
I shall stand by my love.
I shall show the world my love for you.
I shall stand by your side through the good times,
And through the bad times.
I promise to show you my love.
A love like no other kind of love out there.

From this moment.
We shall be Husband and wife.
We will show one another our love.
We shall show the world our love for each other.
And let it shine unto the world.
For our love is very precious.
A love that God gave to each of us.
A love that He told us to show unto one another.
It is true love.

From this moment.
I shall protect you from harm; For I am your knight.
I shall cover you with my wings of love; For I am your Angel.
I shall cover our children from life's harm; For I am their Guardian Angel.
From this moment.
I will show you my soulmate everything about me.
My love, my heart, and my feelings for you.
For our love will shine for all of *eternity*

Travis Applegate

A Poem To Ponder

A winning poem today I read,
Asking where was God today
Nudging feelings for all sufferers,
Questions of the suffering kind.
Will puzzle many a stubborn mind
No answers greater than willingness
In facing all tests more prayerfully.

Christ sacrificed with his life,
His prayers not why, but if it be God's will,
Remove his cup of suffering.

Question not whom God sees fit to save
For he alone sees all our stubbornness,
Many hoping for whatever,
Without a hope to hope alone.

Rachel Taylor

Do You Believe That The World Will End?

According to Jehovah's Witnesses soon this world will end?
Many people think that they are crazy and they do not know what
                                                  they talk about?
Well I was myself a bit sceptical about the Jehovah witnesses but after I start to read the Holy Bible for some time I now come to the
                                          conclusion that they were right.
They do not speak nonsense but they do speak with intelligence.
In many passages of the Holy Bible you will find that this world will
                                                         soon end.
When and how nobody knows anything not even the angels
                                        or Jesus himself.
Only God decides when it is right for him.
But as far as the Jehovah Witnesses are concerned they are all perfect
                                                  in what they say.
They do not tell you any lies
They do preach only the truth of what the Holy Bible says no more
                                                           no less.
They do and say everything that is in the Holy Bible.
It is up to us to believe or not I only can say to all the people of this
                                                      world the truth.
Jehovah Witnesses are the true Christians as we all should be.
If you believe in God or not it is nobody else's business but yourself.
I do personally believe that this world is near the end.

Antonio Martorelli

The Haymakers

Long dreamy days in fields soaked in sunshine,
Bright scarlet poppies and fields full of hay -
High in the heavens a skylark is singing,
Singing to greet the glad summer day.

Lasses in bonnets, blue, pink and yellow
And young laughing lads who whistle all day,
With scythes, rakes and sickles they all work together
Cutting and raking and loading the hay.

Even the horse seems to share the enjoyment -
Raising his head he gives a loud neigh,
Then with a snort amidst all the laughter
He kicks up his hoofs and gallops away.

Time for a break now - more laughter and singing -
A thirst-quenching drink - a quick stolen kiss -
Or maybe a snooze in the shade of a hay-rick -
For those that are weary indeed that is bliss.

But all that is gone now and almost forgotten,
Gone is the laughter and gone is the play -
Gone is the joy of working together -
Instead of all that a machine rules the day.

Margaret Parry

STRAWBERRY FIELDS REVISITED

Let me take you down again
To a place of safety,
To a world
That was a playground,
Where every game
Turned into a ritual
To raise the spirit of fun.

Where mellow winds kissed brows
And dried every tear,
And laughter was the cure
A healing river
That ran through Lovetown,
Images of childhood
A world of spontaneity
When we saw life
And saw it was good.

I see the growth
Of a family tree,
Does it belong to you
It does not belong to me,
For I have been reborn
As an adopted son of the world,
Family ties have been dissolved
In the acidic treatments of time,
I have moved on
Into a wider relationship
With all of humankind,
But still wish to retain
My individuality and childlike simplicity,
I wish to linger in Strawberry Fields
Let me take you down again.

Ian Barton

A Child's Memory

I remember when I was a child,
My father used to take me up for a walk,
To the black bridge, so many steps, so high to look,
But we loved to watch as the old steam trains,
Go passing by all steam and smoky so,
Much puff puff as all steam trains go by.

I remember when I was a child,
My friend Ceris and I walked up The Tumps,
What for? We took our picnic baskets for food for tea,
On the lovely green mountainside so big,
We rolled in turn, right down the mountain tump,
The sun was out, so hot to play but we laughed all day.

I remember when I was a child,
My father would take my for a walk on a sunny day,
Near the farm to take bread, what for?
To feed the horse Blacky his name.
My father would lift me up to pat old Blacky's nose,
And when we were going home Blacky used to look, to say goodbye.

Christine Slurey

VERS LE SOIR

The broad fields of England:
The morning darkened, there came a flash of pain.
The Lord filled me with fire;
Heat of this tested wisdom.

When forests have grown on her northern mountains
Increasing risk of thundery showers;
Sweetness came from the wounds of Christ,
As the dark night winds blew down from London.

There are clouds across the evening:
Dark spires throw a growing shadow.
Are nations only temporary arrangements?
Is there a tyranny of tired old things?

New freshness comes with the dew;
Was it wrong to have known all the answers?
Then they heard on her low coasts
The thunder of an evening wave.

Lorcan O'Connor

LETTING GO

He's leaving behind so many years
of sweat and toil, laughter and tears
he'll be all the talk of the steamie
the latest to go to the wall

he's starting a job on Monday
and oh aye, here's the novelty
for the first time in years
someone else has to worry
about how they are going to pay him

and when this sad day
has become tomorrow's memory
I guess he will look back and say
the hardest part was letting go

so he's moving on starting again
there's been bigger losses at sea
he listens to news of Kosovo
and the plight of the refugee

and knows whatever he stands to lose
at least he had the freedom to choose

Heather Kirkpatrick

CANDLEWICK SWEETHEART

An unopen lullaby seeps from the tears of a flame.
Its gentle light dances a happy jig mournfully
Lament.
    In Love. She loves me not.
The source of my emotions, it flickers a
Naked
flame.
Naked, yet fatal to touch
    In Love. She loves me.
Staying bright, it burns on, wavering peacefully.
    In love. She loves me not
Estella.
    In Love. She loves me.
With one kiss, she blows my Candle out.
    In love? She loves me not.

Rob Herd

Just For Tonight

Just for tonight - take all my cares,
And brush all pain and doubt away.
Please send a little healing, Lord,
To soothe the wounding of the day.
Give me contentment through the dark.
A quiet sleep, rest and repair.
Plant in my heart, new strength and hope
To combat trouble and despair.
So when tomorrow wakes the sky
And I arise to meet the day
Help me to do the best I can
And walk with you along the way.
But until then, wrap me in love.
And keep me safe, though shadows creep.
Just for tonight - shut out the world.
And grant, Oh Lord, the gift of sleep.

William Price

Death On The Beach

Still silent starfish soaking in a rockpool
Lovingly entangled inside each other's fingers
Slightly limp-tinged with a pink hue
Stuck together with coarse crustaceans
Rainbow-like in the summer sun
Little children come to look at you
To catch you in their nets
To watch you squiggle and squirm
But now it's as if
You've just dropped
From the sky
And left to jellify
In a cold rockpool
Without any bubbles.

Barbara King

SURVIVAL

All I want in my eye to fill
Is the sight of an English Shire
Seen from the spry height
Of a comely English hill:
A great and serious green beyond
Broken here and there
By a narrow English river
And, the best, a lively village pond;

The piking paradisewards spires of
First Pious churches,
Hiked just higher than
Their neighbouring trees,
Those beneficent mately associates -
Maybe Oaks and Birches;
Heralds to the other hand
Of centuries formed woodland,
With peaks moving in a very English breeze.

And, through this beat, an out-of-order lane
Dimly winding across the filling plain,
Initiated before Augustine;
Hoof, wheel and simple shoe made:
Now silence walks where the route is allowed to remain;
And its ghosts of travels early
Makes modernists afraid:
The Starting Place of the English Journey.

Emeritus Apollo, above all, is the genteel welkin
Borrowed often by hearty English clouds,
Thick topgallant bulbs of white, sinister at night;
But it's in the sunlight we see their death design,
Unless we're towned, part of the eyes down crowds.

England surrounds us,
Towns and Cities are only in its grounds;
Metropolitan racket cannot drown
What we arose from;
What we try to pull down.

Charles Butler

PRIVATE HEALTH CARE PLAN

The National Health Service was going bust. So I took out a
health care plan.
The salesman who sold it to me. Said you just cannot go wrong
my man.
We have five different levels of care. That you can choose from Sir.
I might have guessed from the beginning. That I should be aware.
Of the small print at the bottom of the page. That's so hard to read.
But the salesman was so persuasive. So I readily agreed.
I took out the platinum five-star plan. For all the family.
But I very soon found out. That it did not cover even me.
For heart transplants. Liver pancreas and the like.
And when I needed them the most. They said push off on your bike.
I've given up my platinum five-star plan. In favour of the NHS.
Because I know I'm going to die. So I will do it on the cheap I guess.

Don Goodwin

SANDSTONE AFTERNOON

Across sandstone walls the beautiful glow of a setting sun
A mystical shade of deepest red
Lifeblood flowing in words seldom said
In the breathless heat of a late summer afternoon
A sky of revelations
Infinite and crystal-blue
The far distant feeling of watching from another room
In brushstroke clouds of life and hope
Eyes mist with tears and wonder
For this moment shall be seen again and again
So too the thought of a schoolyard ringing with bells and laughter
Suddenly silent and watching
Lengthening shadows seem to stretch and yawn
Hands raised to encompass the tender light of unimagined love
The source of beginning and new dawn

Paul Andrew Jones

Enigma: CLIV (b)-?

'Now is the winter of our discontent';
Methinks I've heard that somewhere else before —
This poem neither mocks, nor harm is meant,
'Tis but an essay in a form of yore
And difficult, one finds it, to sustain,
In spite of erudition's thin veneer,
So scrambled are the thoughts of egg-like brain
Which gather to confound the inner ear.
Forsooth I'd like to try another tack,
Yet must I keep my mind set on the goal
And even if intelligence I lack
Should put some shade of meaning to the whole —
Gadzooks! though many like their Bacon boiled,
Or Marlowe, murdered - never Shakespeare , soiled.

J Duncan Warmingham

SUE

So often in my dreams you're there,
My sleeping hours with you I share.
I hear your voice, I see your face,
I feel my heartbeat quicken pace.

Alone through fields and woods we walk,
Or sometimes we just sit and talk.
I often hold you in my arms,
Besotted by your many charms.

As time goes by my thoughts unfold,
So many words remain untold.
So many thoughts, I'd like to share,
To tell you how I really care.

But night-time ends to spoil my bliss,
With not so much as a goodbye kiss.
Returning to my daily grind,
My dreams have faded from my mind.

Your image still remains a while,
Those warming eyes and cheeky smile.
And though I often think of you,
I know that dreams do *not* come true.

But more importantly in the end,
I always want to be your friend.
So whenever you are feeling down,
You know I'll always be around . . .

Steve Harris

CIRCLE OF LIFE

Where does it start, show me the end
a world is so round, the circle my friend
the shape of the globe, the form of the sun
the fullness of moon, my story's begun

The roundness of belly, the birth of my head
seed from the ball, the breasts which I fed
a half circle smile, the centre of love
the cycle of life from the halos above

Semi-round rainbows, a square floppy disc
my body forms whole, surrounded by risk
the girth of the family, the link in the chain
round window eyes to see you again

Spinning top hearts and dizzy romance
wheel of good fortune, social class dance
And now to the ring, the solid love band
I jump through your hoop to a roundabout land

Life is so round, death is too square
corners so sharp, the illness unfair
the rectangle coffin, a long straight face
look to the sun and life's circle embrace.

Deborah Morris

SAD PAD

They sit around the edge, just staring into space,
Waiting for the routine - again to take place,
All of them stopped thinking for themselves,
Like statues - reminiscent of gnomes and elves,
That they are like this - I'm not surprised,
As they have become - institutionalised,
Elderly they may be - but still human beings,
None really concerned with their inward feelings
Up in the morning - deposited in a chair,
Then almost forgotten - as most don't care,
Just like they - the staff's routine,
Has enveloped them too - until all have been,
Lost in space - in a place down here,
All folk who have families - who hold them dear,
Almost zombies - obeying out-of-date rules,
Until everyone in the building - finish up like fools!

John L Wright

You

You have given so much, loved so much, been caring thoughtful,
                                                      also kind.
You have walked your path in life knowing you were loved which is
                                                 happiness to find.
You have travelled many roads in your endeavours but have
                                            never been alone.
Because you have been a homemaker made a welcome place
                                              called home.
There have been times of trauma you have dealt with,
supported sometimes with others by your side.
But life wherever you did reside.
You have seen beauty of nature's seasons, felt cold of winter days.
Lived its hours, days, weeks, years, had your past, looked to your future
So many happenings have paved your ways.
Being fulfilled in feelings, being fulfilled in one's heart.
Because forever we travel on our road in life to end from start.

Victoria Joan Theedam

I'M THE MAN

I'm the man born from a woman who was sent to the gates
of raging war
To sunless places and wild jungles, over rocky hills and
fruitless valleys I had never seen before
In my youthful hands of innocence they placed a menacing
machine gun
And clenching their ice cold fists and raising their intense voices
my commanding officers retorted
'Show the bloody bastards no mercy son'
So with spirits high and adventures to cease I marched in song with
companion and friend
Until we descended upon the stained darkness of the blood-hungry
battlefields of hell where we were to defend
And through the torn hearts and ravaged heads of many rows of
shrieking and shattering bullets we sent
And like a crimson curse bombs from the sky we dropped until nothing
but a limelight of twilight devastation and fire lay ahead
And with my bloody hands I fired wildly with my machine gun,
sinking both child and adult alike into the bitter ground which
became their graves
I have seen and felt bruised ribs of pain in the quivering limbs and
stricken eyes of both companion and enemy
I have felt emotions to which there is no cure or remedy
Now my mind starved with destruction I walk home down
half-unknown roads to the worshipping cries of a
drum-beating ceremony
Welcomed with open arms by unfamiliar faces I have never seen
before but yet consider me a hero
I'm the man ashamed to be born from a mother
Who went into the great wild world and drenched his hands in the
murdered blood of his sisters and brothers

Saheda Khan

The Reluctant Visitor

I hear humming outside my window
Drawing me in, if I would dare.
Go away, go away, I know you are there.
Let me sleep until tomorrow.

Why do you play these mind games?
I know you are more advanced than we.
Even humans can be psychic; we sense we feel we be.
Let me sleep until tomorrow.

If there is something you want
It's good manners to ask.
Why not share your knowledge and set me a task.
Let me sleep until tomorrow.

Are you waiting for me?
I'm resourceful and clever; I think on my feet.
For our mutual benefit, I think we should meet.
Let me dream until tomorrow.

My innermost being is full of feeling,
You're light years ahead but aeons behind.
Computers rule your tiny mind.
Let me dream until tomorrow.

We're all mind covered in matter,
What matters is that we all mind.
Use your heads, trust your hearts, just be kind.
Let me wake to a new beyond.

T M Wright

A Man And His Willie

A man and his willie, there's much more there than just a link,
Not only a pleasurable tool at times, it is the way in which they think.
A man and his willie or his middle leg that he calls Dick,
Always reaching his destination, far too often and far too quick.
A man and his willie, his inspiration and his drive,
So testosterone dependant, sadly upon this us women thrive.
A man and his willie, large, small, quantity matters, yes, it's true,
You can bet they'll be comparing at the urinals in the loo.
A man and his willie, *need* I repeat it anymore?
We spend a lifetime trying to understand them, when we do really
                                              know the score.
So when you need to reach a man, food's not the way to his heart,
                                              now silly,
Appeal to his sense of better judgement, his common sense and
                                              call for Willie.

Rachael Hewett

PHOBIAS

Phobias start with a tiny worry
And grow until you feel sorry.
Hands get washed in a ritual cycle
Gets on the nerves of husbands like Michael.
Housework done till hands are raw
Then done again many times more.
Exhausted, weary, but cannot stop
Another bottle of bleach to go on top.
Hands bleeding, sweat runs in the eye
Tears well up, want to stop, but can't try.
On and on goes this daily hell
Oh how we long to make our minds well.
Count the numbers in our head
It's daybreak sometimes before we get to bed.
Blood phobia also makes our life hell
As anything touched by blood must be washed well.
Can't touch the stuff or be near
We are driven by this deep fear.
Isolated in this strange phobia world
No one understands how our brains unfurl.
They tease, get irritable or leave the house
As we turn more and more into a mouse.
The deep heat that arises from within us
To others it's just a lot of fuss.
Toilets cleaned till they gleam
We get upset when others have been.
Scrubbing, washing, cleaning, germs must go
This is the life for the sufferer as nobody knows.

Jean Rendell

A Woman's World

A woman's world is a strange place
Of which none dream.
A woman's contentment is a happy home.
Children and grandchildren filling her day
With a man earning the pay.
But is it so?
Many women want to work
Especially when the kids are grown.
How often does the man relax
Whilst his woman skivvies, just for him?
Washing, shopping, cleaning, making, painting
And countless chores beside.
But what's that mark upon her arm, her face, her chest?
No - nothing said. No complaints made
Why?
All for quiet, all for peace.
Stop!
If accidental we'd understand.
Battered women. Battered lives.
Often known but little done.
A woman's life isn't always happy.
So often it's left to her to see it through,
To maintain unity of contented family
Which all dream about but seldom find.

T B Smith

The Jacket

A sports jacket I once had
Formally belonged to my Dad,
Of a tweed material that was white
Its colour held fast and was very bright.
To wear it was comfortable and warm
And it kept out the cold and winter's storm,
Its leather buttons were brown and shiny
And rather large and far from tiny.
In it I looked quite tidy and smart
Wearing it warmed the cockles of my heart,
I carried it on my shoulders with pride
Pride that I did not want to hide.
The threads were thick and well bound
And the workmanship was solid and sound,
Cut and tailored by a firm that was old
For a price that was reasonable all told.
Only the pockets needed some repair
And were done by myself with great care,
The memory of that jacket I will ever treasure
For wearing it gave me very great pleasure.

W Fred Tabaczynski

THE BIRTHDAY CAKE

It's John and David's 50th birthday
I've had to make a cake
It took a lot of mixing
I thought my back would break
I got it in the oven
It took six hours to bake
And now I've got to ice it
And put on almond paste

I asked my best friend Pamela
To help me ice this cake
'Oh no' she said 'get on with it
A good job you will make'

Well I pleaded and I bribed her
She kept on saying 'no'
I pestered and I pestered
Till she said 'Go on we'll have a go'

She told me quite plainly
All the things and all the stuff
I had to carry from Barnsley
It made me huff and puff

So all the things were gathered
And when I wasn't there
She almond and she iced this cake
My friend beyond compare
Pam Brown

__Kathy French__

WESLEY THE WASP

Young Wesley the wasp is the bane of my life
In spring summer and autumn he makes my life hell
His sole intention in his small life seems to be
To put his sting somewhere in me
He likes to see me run and shout and try my best to hide away
I've hit him with a newspaper and squashed him flat
I've stood on him and even flushed him down the bog
But for strange reasons and powers unknown to me
He is reincarnated in the blink of one's eye
Sometimes he brings his mates, he always knows where I am
He can find me in a crowd of thousands, how I just can't tell
Now young Wesley the wasp must have a charmed life
Every year he's about, this wasp never ever dies
He has built-in radar and he tunes it in on me
I would like to pin him on a card in a mucky museum
And see if he likes the point he gives me every year.

The wasp is known in North America as a yellow jacket.
To me in the North of England it's known as a sharp-arsed one.

Dohmnall Le Gai

DRUIDS HARBOUR

Oh yes! I knew the Druids Harbour,
Often walked the rocky shore.
Watched the tide rush round the headland.
Felt the chill wind from the moor.

Oh yes! I knew the Druids Harbour,
From the point they set the sail.
Goods and dreams for distant dwellings,
Searching for their Holy Grail.

Oh yes! I knew the Druids Harbour.
The rituals in that sacred wood.
There the novices learnt the mysteries.
And against the Roman phalanx stood.

And folks met at the Druids Harbour.
Of what wonders would you hear?
Learn of wizard, dragon and saga,
The legend of Arthur and Guinevere.

I often dream of Druids Harbour,
Lanterns bobbling in the sea's darkest night.
A small boat breaking on the horizon,
Under the winter suns pale light.

A caravan park now scars Druids Harbour.
Burgers, chips and amenity blocks.
Plastic things for a plastic people,
On the holy ground of Druids Docks.

So come with me to Druids Harbour,
Journey back through all the years.
A life more meaningful and romantic.
Our golden past, have no fears.

Brian Haswell

HMP

As I cast my mind back the years just fall away.
I think of all those things I'd turn to you and say.
Me and you we were inseparable then,
But my way of life drove us apart time and time again.

Wherever I smelt perfume
I'd expect you to enter the room
The way you were back then.
But all I'm left with are the memories of you.

Your beautiful face, your style, your grace
It's those little things about you I'm going to miss.
The way you would apply make-up to your face,
Also how you would style your hair.

You would pout your lips, turn to me and smile.
I would give just anything to see once more your face.
Now you're just a memory, a part of my past, ancient history,
Like 1066, the past is the past.

Back into my mind those memories of you blast,
It's a pity I've lost you but I will not ever forget
A love like you.

Jonathon Covington

My Wife

My wife shares my ambitions
Is proud when I succeed,
And in times of indecision
All her faith is guaranteed.
She's ever there when needed
She helps in all I do.
The one I love with all my heart,
Ever wonderful - ever you.

Denys George Hill

THE OLD WOODEN SHED

Built with pride was the old wooden shed,
the tools all inside once shone bright with newness.
Each used to work hard with their owner each day,
transforming their garden, putting all in array.
The lawn was all cut, flowers grew there with pride,
no weeds to be seen, it was a gardener's paradise.
But years have now passed and that owner has died.
The weeds have taken over, that garden's lost all its pride.
Those tools are now rusty, that shed's rotting away,
its door creaks out stories of those happy old days.

Sandra Brisck

LOOKING FOR A PATH

No birds with broken wings can fly,
Or distraught spirits reach the sky.
Life on the streets where souls are found,
Lost in a jungle of bricks and stones,
Looking for a path a way to their home.
Self worth disappears like a puff of smoke.
Human kindness, their only hope.

M Rossi

WRONGFUL ATTRACTION

As we were introduced
Our eyes locked in a gaze,
Is this what they mean by love at first sight,
Or is it a passing phase?

Feelings towards another man
I know is so unfair,
But when he speaks and when he smiles
I do not honestly care.

Thoughts of him never leave my head
He's on my mind all day,
But without my partner I'd never see him again,
As he lives some distance away.

Emotions such as these
I have never experienced before,
But if the truth was ever revealed
I'd be out of the door for sure.

I know that a decision has to be made,
I can't go on living a lie.
I must risk losing one and all,
It's come time to say goodbye.

Laura McAulay

Millennium

Will you come with the breeze,
On the night of all nights,
Or like a soft whisper,
By the dawns of early light,
Or on a white steed,
With a thunderous roar,
To light up the heavens,
Like never before.
Or maybe as sun,
From the east starts to glow,
You'll ride on the stars,
And the world it will know.
As the shadow of truth,
Passes over the land,
Heralded in
By the angelic band,
And darkness might fall,
Or the earth set on fire,
As man's sins are counted,
The waters rise higher.
Or maybe that night,
Will pass into dawn,
And the truth, still out there,
And another day born,
And only a fool,
Or maybe a clown,
Will make any sense,
As the stars look on down.
And to those who gave vigil,
On that special night,
Friend, God's in His Heaven,
And the world is all right.

J Brohee

The Book

It's only an old man standing in the dark
Watching the people on the street slowly depart
Back to their wives and families and cosy home
Leaving the old man all on his own.
For thirty years he had been on the street
No bed, no money and very little to eat
He had his dreams, a lifetime ago
But suddenly those dreams stopped to grow.
He had a wife, two sons, a business of his own
But all day and late nights, he was never at home.
His wife took the children and started a new life
He knew that without them he would never survive.
He started to drink and that long slow dive
Into obscurity never feeling alive.
Now he walked the streets of this great city
Never asking for help, nor looking for pity.
A bottle of meths in the pocket of his army coat,
His other possession was a book that someone wrote.
He shambles off farther into the dark, dank night
Doing all he could to keep out of sight.
Frayed trouser and jacket, one hand clasping the book
The street cleaner found him in a backstreet nook
Meths bottle empty, but he was not drunk
He died in the night from the cold and the rain
No-one on this earth would ever know his pain
But still in his hand he held onto his book,
There was a tear in his eye, if the dustmen had but looked
And then they would have seen in his hand his ever faithful book,
The Bible he had carried for more than thirty years.
Now the good Lord above wiped away the old man's tears.

R Davidson

THE RACE

Now that this race of life is almost run
I wonder was it lost, or was it won.
At the start of it, the obstacles seemed high
What strength of purpose, always made me try
To overcome, and in so doing make
A firmer hold on life, I learned to take
I do believe my help came from above
Along with hope, and faithfulness, and love
I never doubted what I had to do,
And looking back the errors made were few,
How can we judge? When time itself is gone
And what the prize, if race is ever won,
The sweet forgetfulness of heavenly bliss,
The nothingness of life's last lingering kiss
Or is this just an interlude of pace
A further leap into a different space
Where time itself no longer is to be
And I though life, was real reality
I cannot say, for I am yet about
Winning this race, and trying not to shout,
Take care, and have a heed for what you see
This life you know, beyond is yet to be.

Edna Hunt

FAREWELL RABIN

On Saturday night, 4th November 1995
The world was shocked with terror.
Let not the crowds hang on Mount Zion
Let not the sea stop to give her fish.
Let not the sun stop to shine
On the city of David.
May the bloodstains on the ground
Remain a perpetual symbol of peace.
Our cries have reached Horeb, and
Zion, and the desert on our
Side have become tears of river.
May we not hear the gunshots again!
May the traitors live to regret their deed.
Adios Rabin, goodbye, and may
God give you perpetual rest and peace.
We salute you, great noble
Laureate of peace.
Let not the crowds hang on Mount Zion,
Let not the sea stop to give her fish.
Let not the sun stop to shine on
The city of David.
May the God of peace
Reign in Israel.

James Peter King Appiah

BLUE EYES

I look at the ocean,
And think of your eyes
Eternal depth,
As blue as the sky's.
I gaze at the sunset,
And see your face
Beauty that no other
Could ever replace.
I feel a light breeze,
And recall your touch.
A softness that healed
When times got rough.
One day I hope
To recover these treasures.
Should I win back your heart,
I will keep it forever.

Richard Higgins

The Legend Of Jerai-Shul

Go carefully!
The way is rough and the air is thin.
We are the first to tread
These dusty corridors
In twice ten thousand years!

What were they like
Those darkling ones,
The folk of Jerai-Shul?
That carven shape on the crumbling wall
If only it could talk!

What dreadful deed was this,
What unsung story told?
Of the broken sword,
Through broken bones
Of some, once powerful, lord.

See that stain on the marble floor
Where once a bronze axe lay?
And whose fair hand
Last touched the latch
Of that, half-open, door?

Outside, a beast upon a plinth,
An empty, riderless back.
Did family weep
Or kinfolk seek
For one lost far from home?

Questions posed and answers none,
Out of a silent world.
From time gone by,
To time that is,
The years have flowed like the sea.

This haunted place, its secrets holds
For no one knows the time,
When those who came
Removed and left
The ruin called Jerai-Shul.

Dana Adler

WHEN THE DAFFODILS BLOOM

You are close to me when the daffodils bloom,
So near, I see love in your eyes.
Sharing the fresh green beauty of spring,
And the light of the clear blue skies.

Secrets shared of our childhood days:
What we did, and where we went.
Parallel in so many ways
Of moments that are 'heaven-sent.'

In our mind they safely lie,
Till we have a need to recall;
Memories of some distant day
That mean so much to us all.

How precious these moments, and
The mind where they're stored.
For our many blessings
We give thanks to the Lord.

God in his wisdom gave us our mind,
To store these memories in.
What would we do without it?
We wouldn't know where to begin!

Gold in the air when the daffodils bloom.
Close you stand beside me.
Sharing the love we will always share,
And the generous wealth of God's bounty.

Stan Davenport

A Meal Of An Ode

The chips didn't move, the fish was fried
The meal needed more, but what?
Then, as if by magic appeared on the side
A pile of peas, all shiny and hot.

These peas did quiver and they did quake
All knowing what they had in store,
But their leader shouted 'For goodness sake
Let's run - come on head for the door'

The rest of the peas watched in fear
As their leader yelled 'Oh yike'
Then putting on his leather gear
He jumped on his motorbike.

He tore round and round over the table mat
Showing wheel spins and balancing to me
I would give him his freedom - I'm nice like that
And I will call him my little escape-pea.

Lesley Tomlinson

There Is A Wonderful Beginning

Hands on the wheel and steer
'Blue Water Park'
A fabulous start to this year!
Shop till we drop, all under one roof!
Prices to suit, for the not so well off,
Plenty of course for the rich and aloof.
A privilege for me to live so close.
Five minutes I'm home and indoors
Who wouldn't boast.

Jackie Gaish

LIFE

What's the meaning of my life,
I need to know the purpose of me.
The fantasies I have of the future
The battle of who I'm going to be.

It's hard 'cause I wonder,
If there's a point to live.
If God gave me this gift,
Something to repay him, to give.

I've got to be special,
To teach the world, I'm here,
I want to help, to have a purpose,
To help those who fear.

I'm curious to know what'll happen,
I need to know, God why I'm here.
I need the world to know I exist,
I need to know, do you hear?

Louise Gough

Sweet Dreams

Well we were in our element,
When chocolate town was discovered.
The smell made our mouths water,
Everything was completely covered.
White chocolate, milk and plain,
To meet required tastes of everyone.
Candy trees that lined the roads,
Made a canopy of shade from the sun.

Greeted with open arms by townsfolk,
Ready to show off their spectacular sights.
With lemonade sparkling in the fountain,
Were you allowed to eat or drink these delights?
Sugar-coated flowers decorated flower beds,
Candyfloss bushes we found more tempting.
Then we were led to the toffee hotel,
Where it was buzzing as lunch was commencing!

Ordering chocolate chips and candied eggs,
With ice cream and lemonade to follow,
Tea, marshmallow sandwiches plus chocolate cake,
Wow! Wonder what's on the menu for tomorrow.
Then strawberry milkshakes before our goodbyes,
But feeling green, finding it hard to swallow.
Suddenly I awake, to my horror to find,
An empty chocolate wrapper on my pillow!

Ann Beard

Ghosts

Lots of folk have seen them looking
like you and me,
making sure their relatives are safe
as they can be,

Once the children's grandfather appeared
to me to say,
'If all of you go in that car I'll see
you all today.'

Then I saw a soldier sitting on my bed,
it was my father's photograph I'd seen
when still spoon fed.

In a great Cathedral as I prayed for one day,
high up in a long walkway they put on a display.

I saw a priest with a gold cross, altar boys close behind,
my prayers were answered for that day
which I thought rather kind.

Animals can see ghosts, we had a cat that stared,
into a corner of a room where pipe smoke often flared.

We may all see our ancestors, our lives might never end,
there is a lot for us to learn to try to comprehend.

People are afraid of the thought of being near,
such boundless knowledge shaking all the
concepts they thought clear.

We're on the edge of something great,
a real millennium treat,
the inner world will be explored, nature's
own heart's strong beat.

Jean Paisley

WORLD WITHOUT END?

Look after this world
For it has served you well,
Down all the long ages
Since the dawn of man.
As a mother feeds a baby
So it has nourished you,
With every breath of air you breathe
And every crop you grow.
Where every golden sunset
Promises tomorrow's dawn,
And every shining rainbow
Proclaims that rain has come.
Where season follows season
Without man's intervention,
Look after this world
For it has served you well.

Look after this world
For there's nowhere else to live,
Nowhere else to walk sure-footed
With your spirit high and free.
Nowhere to feel the sun's warm rays
Or winter's icy touch,
To catch the spray from foaming tide
Or dance on dew soaked grass.
Nowhere to bathe in moonlight
Or watch a shooting star,
To see night's velvet darkness
Turn peacefully to morn.
Every generation
Leaves a legacy for the next,
So look after this world
For there's nowhere else to live.

Look after this world
For it is all you have,
To hold you in the universe
Among a million stars.
All you have to bind you
To those who've gone before,
Who worked and left their best in trust
For you to carry on.
Though the earth is yours to cherish
For your allotted span,
To keep a world which has no end
Means help from everyone.
For the future of your children
And for your children's children,
Look after this world
For it is all you have.

Patricia J Harding

I Surrender

I surrender to God's will,
I surrender to love and tenderness,
I surrender to health and beauty,
I surrender to peace and harmony.

I surrender to forgiveness and truth,
I surrender to hope and wisdom,
I surrender to joy and celebration,
I surrender to eternity and Jesus.

Kenneth Mood

BRADFORD'S COMPLEXION

Bradford has changed, in fact we've become metropolitan,
with its citizens, now so cosmopolitan,
Life has become fuller,
with its stonework now clean, it may be seen in full technicolor!

If you have a car,
You may travel far.
Seeking somewhere to park it,
So for somewhere to shop.
You may now shop
at the supermarket!

When viewing cricket , a different sight,
No longer garbed in all white.
Now played at night, becomes a panorama
with the players to be seen in their pyjamas.

Benny Howell

MY RABBIT

Two tall ears, a little button nose,
A round fluffy tail, she's the best one I know,
She makes a funny noise that makes me happy,
If she ran away it makes me sad straight away.

Tina Eccles

The Modern Executioner

It was pits and mostly foundries
in my hometown all around.
Now there isn't anywhere
those styles of work are found.

They are now no longer viable
In this modern day and age.
So their workforce is now idle
and do not earn a wage.

Some men who are just forty
No longer have a living.
Their family life is nothing now
with the benefits they are given.

This is the tragedy of today
With this sad and woeful tale
But when you have progression
Older methods all grow stale.

Lachlan Taylor

How Can We Tell?

The book of Revelation informs us all,
What to expect at the final knell,
Diseases and wars and deadly pall,
The problem is, 'How can we tell?'

For man has gone so far from the Lord,
In filth and mire he has made his bed,
Innocents are beaten while crowds applaud,
While old folk tremble and wish they were dead.

Diseases tear at the heart of man,
Aids and Cancers and even worse,
But this has nothing to do with God's plan,
It's man's evil heart that has become diverse.

We have chosen Mammon as our sovereign Lord,
Our greed leads us into war and strife,
We covert goods we can't afford,
Thirty pieces of silver won't spare a life.

The prophets gave us Revelation as a guide,
So we could expect the return of God's Son,
But even before the human race can be tried,
We have brought destruction down on everyone.

So unless this generation turns back to God,
One thing is for sure, we are bound for Hell,
But one thing I worry about as onward I plod,
If hell begins now - how can we tell?

Bill Hayles

ALBATROSS

Cruising along so idly
Like a cloud that won't bring rain
Like a promise that won't bring pain
I'll try not to block the sun
As I glide by without a care
I'm just drifting along
Just cruising alone in the air

Miles away from any other land
Like a dog that's got no chain
Like a child that's got no shame
I'll try not to be cruel
As I scale the walls of life
Miles away from trouble
Just cruising alone free of strife

Sun rises now from the ocean
The water's so deep and blue
The sky all round's the same too
But I know where I'm going
I'll always find my way
As I rise now with the sun
That pours light into each day

Wandering lonely so high
Like the rings of Saturn in space
Like the wings of a loved one in chase
I'll lower myself back down
Finished cruising in solitary skies
As I sink now with the day
Dreams wandering off in the night

Rodger Moir

FLOWER GIRL

Not yet in full bloom
Is our flower girl
Surrounded by colour
In harmony with another
Smile shared freely
Never empty
Magnetic eyes melt many
Viewed frequently
Personality appealing
Shall hardly wilt
Blossom instead
Elegance grows not to shed

Alan Jones

The Awards

Have you seen them in their penguin suits
All lining up for photo shoots.
All the women in long sparkly gowns
That cost hundred and thousands of pounds.
With egos as big as their mouths
They really do love themselves.
'Oh, you must remember me,
I've been in films and on TV.'
They don't actually say it
They just know how to play it.
They sit at round tables, filling their faces
Drinking wine in big expensive places.
'The nominations are,' there usually are three,
Two from the BBC and one from ITV.
'The winner is,' the announcer says
They're all sitting there trying to guess
'For her part in that wonderful television play.'
She climbs on stage, and doesn't know what to say
She's probably sat at her table rabbiting on.
Now on stage, and the words have gone.
When she does finally speak
It all sounds a bit feeble and weak.
She thanks everybody else for the award
'I could never have done it without you' and they all applaud.
If she's a very good actress, she will force a tear
Then we all feel sorry for the egotistical dear.

B Page

WHEN I WAS YOUNG

When I was young the girls at school
talked about fashion and pop groups
They reviewed last night's TV
Discussed new tapes, new films to see

Now they talk of boys and sex
Taking precautions, trouble with the ex
Their gossip is polluted with HIV
Condoms and the blame is never on me

I never heard a word about drugs
What were they? I wondered
In my late teens I heard about Pot
Heroin and LSD, speed the lot

I wouldn't want to be young again
With drugs, crime and sex to inflict its pain
When I was young I said no to a fag
Nowadays I'd be offered a 'drag'
It used to be tobacco they smoked behind the shed
Now it is pot and some are near dead.

P Edwards

SECRET LOVE

Across the room our glances met
Deeply into your eyes I gazed
Seeing the love for me you held
That neither time nor distance could erase.
Still I knew that we must part
Your tender kisses I would no more receive.
Love for you would stay deep in my heart
Though your loving caresses I would not feel.
I pass you by whene'er we meet
I look at you but dare not greet.
We who shared such tender feelings
We pass as strangers in the street.

Polina Belle McCann

Corner Shop

Little, crumbling shop on the corner
Of a grimy inner London street,
A ghost of its former self,
With a cardboard cut-out Bovril ad in the window,
And half adozen tins on the shelf.
Over the door a sign revealing:
'The Regal Emporium -
Stanley Owen licensed to . . .' the rest lost in paint peeling,
Victim of a recessionary moratorium.

Stan Owen still hangs about it
For the rare customer or two,
And wonders, to entice back business,
What the hell he can possibly do.

Once it was a handy place when folk ran out of milk or bread,
Or needed fags late in the evening . . . 'Open most hours', Stan said.
And he knew everyone local,
Always said the expected thing,
Like 'Any better news of the missus?'
Or 'Very sad about Harry Pring,'
Even 'Winter draws on, eh, Mrs Dodd?'
('I have *not*, Stanley Owen, you cheeky sod!')
He'd politely ask how the Vicar was,
Reaching for his favourite Three Nuns,
Patiently weigh sticks of liquorice
For the kids, bag them two jam buns.
Nothing seemed too much trouble,
Customers always (well, usually) right.
Though Stan wouldn't handle sticky hubble-bubble,
And closed early every Sunday night.

Then one day in came a Film Director
Who was making a Victorian thriller.
Seeing the Regal, he'd immediately gushed,
'The perfect place! An absolute killer!'
Could he, please, he begged Stan Owen,
Shoot some scenes in his beautiful shop?
Dead keen was that man on verité -
Studio sets were just no cop.

Terms agreed, the designer appeared,
With zeal like His Highness of Wales,
Refurbished the shop, threw out the lino,
Buffed the mahogany counter and old brass scales.
Then in trooped a mighty army of extras
In their assorted Victorian gear:
Labourers, businessmen, housewives, maids -
Typical clients of yesteryear.
And that famous actor (you know - *him*)
Stood, like Stan, slicing ham and hacking
And weighing and most expertly packing
To sell to that actress (you know - *her*).
The Regal Emporium rang with voices and laughter,
The doorbell went ping! The cash register ching!
For Stan it felt like happy-ever-after.

Three days later ended the Regal's resurrection.
Director and crew and extras too
Went off in their different directions.
Now the crumbling little shop on the corner
Of a grimy London street
Wears a large, crudely-lettered billboard
Like a mournful great winding sheet,
Joining the national, joyless chorus
That sounds over hill, heath and vale,
Announcing (is it England? ourselves?) *'For Sale.'*

Adrian Vale

GYPSY BRIDE

She walks with grace,
Over the wooden bridge.
The flowing stream -
Gurgling beneath her.

She skips through the fields,
And the meadows fresh and free.
Her spirit escapes -
In the land so wild.

Back to the wagon,
Her home and heart.
Bathing in the glowing moonlight -
The Gypsy Bride.

Stephanie Reynolds (12)

THE CHOICE

Let me tell you about dambed land;
It is a ground on the outskirts of the
City - filled with old cans and prams
Cycle wheels and bits of rusted
Cars - old rotting wood - not very
Pretty. In fact it's filthy: even dogs
Won't sleep there anymore - only tramps
Down-and-outs - the alcoholic poor.

There are two routes that go there by
Way of into town - the other
Much longer - some more distance
Around the edge and leading into
Green lush countryside, sparkling
Rivers-moss and sedge.
Which way will you take then, is the
Question left unsaid.

David Hazlet

FEELING HUNGRY

When you're feeling hungry
Time can go by so slowly,
Like when I'm out shopping
With me mum.

I say, 'I'm hungry'
She says, 'You've just eaten'

I say again, 'But I'm still hungry'
She says again, 'But you've just eaten'

'Well I don't know, it must be the cold,
But me belly feels like a doughnut with a hole.'

Claire Louise Carter

Morning Thoughts

Seek a fresh goal every day.
Look on all things new.
Show a smile along the way.
Let happiness shine through.
Don't give up, when your plans fail,
Make another start.
I keep a trust, if hope is frail,
And faith within the heart.
Set aside, a time to care.
And then you'll find it's true.
A kindness passed around to share
Will be returned to you!

William Price

THE HAND OF DESTINY

The Hand of Destiny from the wings of her stage *beckons*
Those who would travel as *millennium* brides
A battle of wits with *nations* as pawns
Throws, this *globe* as we *know it* among *'thorns'*
But! What *holds* all schemers and jugglers *back?*
Is 'supremacy' over *all* 'they' will ever lack
Let us in *honesty* seek to be *worth*while
Let others, *'push'* forward *not* knowing toil
'Standing' in the wings of progress 'God's smile'
We learn of many *'important'* things
The *quiz* that finds them wanting
While he of *'no'* academic fame
Solves this and *that,* knowledge a flame.

Jarzie

THE GIFT

A million bells rang in her dream,
Declaring at last she was free!
Until she woke up to a very loud scream,
'All of you! . . . come with me!'
Yet by her bed was this precious gift . . .
From a girl of tender years;
Scrolled from her head - that no tyrant can shift,
Though led away in tears!

'Evil can never exult over man -
Though it sometimes seems that way . . .
Good will result despite any vile plan!
Throughout eternity.'

Tom Ritchie

A Purple Ocean

Rushing, rolling, rising,
the purple ocean sings
with purple undercurrents
and turning swirling pinks.
The twisting purple ocean
with purple waves of lust,
dancing under starlight
a glowing reddish blush.
A wrestling sea of love,
so violent, so still,
a purple sea of passion
waiting just to spill.
The hissing purple ocean
tightly hugs the beach,
kissing sparkling shingle
as it rolls out of reach.
An empty sea of purple
so full of day and night,
an ocean of devotion
sings in the soft moonlight.

Craig Shuttleworth

April Showers

Ice-cold till March,
Now getting warmer,
Looking forward to a fabulous summer.

But just be careful,
Wearing nowt but summer gear,
For the season of heat is not quite here.

You're looking cool,
Feeling as big as a castle tower,
Then comes along an April shower.

Now you're soaking, wet through,
There's nothing you can do,
Nature has made an April fool out of you.

Philip Trivett

A Hat Stand-Off

They went into the tea room. The finest place to meet
Dressed up from head to toe, amongst society's elite

An elegant glance about the room. And disaster! There she sat
A woman dressed to kill, in the very self-same hat.

For a miserable ten minutes she sat stiff and drank her tea
Thinking big signs saying 'matching' were put up for all to see

Then she thought, I'll make a joke of it, for there's nothing to be said
So she caught the woman's eye and she pointed to her head

She gave a little smile and raised a small iced bun
A playful invitation to join her in the fun

The woman's face stayed frozen, like ice on an Arctic bay
She didn't see the joke at all and quickly turned away

How silly! Why not see the joke? What else was there to do?
She gave her one more chance to laugh about it too

A finger to the temple. A smile, a shake of the head
The woman, frozen, caught her eye. The joke went down like lead

Back home she thought how tiresome, to be so serious like that
But in the hallway mirror saw, she'd worn a different hat!

P Grubb

THE COMPLETE FOOL

It had been a busy day
So it was with great relief
At night to kick my shoes off
Till I stared in disbelief -

Oh misery, catastrophe!
I nearly blew a fuse
When I realised with horror
I'd been wearing *two odd shoes!*

Where had I been, and who had seen?
My heart began to quail.
Then laughter shook, the fool I'd looked -
I'd been to a jumble sale!

A Wilkinson

An April Fool

The salesman came to call
Was I such an April Fool.
Sold me a cordless iron
Signed his name of Lenny the Lion.
Gave me an apple without a core
A lock for a left-hand door.
Rainbow paint in an empty can
Fat for a non-stick pan.
A single meal for two
Tea at the local zoo.
David Beckham's football sock
Thank God it is twelve o'clock.

Colin Allsop

APRIL IN UPPERMILL

Apologies to Uppermill for causing long delays
We love your charming village and its quaint little ways.
Our Fiat threw a wobbly and jammed your narrow roads,
Which is why we ignored you when you told us where to go.
But policing in Uppermill, by car and van and bike
Made our breakdown on zig-zags a motoring delight!
Praise by the boatload for the knight who saved our day
Thank you, AA Relay Man, for towing us away
And to verbalising morons who got right up my nose
Thanks for the grist in abundance from a Lancastrian Rose!

Betty Lightfoot

By Word Of Mouth

Filming a scene on outdoor location
I was the cause of amused consternation
When the Director advised me to shout -
Obeying his order - my false teeth flew out.
As 'Action' was called - giving volume demanded
My 'choppers' (scene-stealing) on green grass safe landed.

Frances Cox

AN APRIL SHOWER

The moon shines through looking all forlorn
Tired moonbeams flop onto my new-cut lawn.
A big moonbeam strikes - like a Moses' wand
Lighting up the lilies in my old fishpond.

Like a warning finger from a long-lost mate
It silhouettes me - leaning on my garden gate.
Four hours, three days since you stormed on your way
I've waited and waited for you - every day!

Hoping and hoping, you - in the distance I'd sight
All I've ever really done is wasted every day - every night!
No-one could ever love you the way I do
But you still up and left me, you're so untrue!

I used to wake up every morning to a bright new sun
And gaze in admiration at the new love I'd won.
My heart's grown sad, it's no longer funny
You've run off with him. Taken all of my money!

Four days I've spent here. My heart full of hope
I realise now - I'm just a first class dope!
What hurts the most, what 'kills' the worst
Is that you 'up and left' me - on April the first!

Bob Hessey

APRIL FOOL'S DAD

Me and my dad were sitting down watching TV
While my sister Charanjit was writing a letter
It was to my dad saying that the queen wanted to visit him.
My dad got the letter and nearly had a heart attack
My sister Charanjit said 'April Fool's Dad'
My dad was embarrassed.

Darshan Marawha (12)

Gavin Butterworth's Coming To Tea

Remember the time, it's half-past three,
Gavin Butterworth's coming to tea.
He sent you a note, he'll be coming by four
We know you can't wait 'til he knocks on the door.
You've cut all the sandwiches, so neat and precise
Your chocolate cake's yummy, can't we have a slice?
You've remembered the corkscrew and chilled out the wine
Now everything's perfect, we're sure you'll be fine.
Everything's scrumptious, you're beautifully dressed,
For Gavin Butterworth, it must be the best!
You're all of a jitter, your cheeks blushing red
He 'phoned up this morning, and that's what he said.
We know you keep asking 'Are we really sure?'
But he definitely told us he'd be 'round here by four.
We can see by the look on your face you're delighted,
We really can't wait, because we all feel excited.
Five minutes to go now, so we'll wait outside
When four o'clock comes 'round, then we'd better hide.
We expect he'll be early, rather than late
He knows he's expected, do you know the date?
One last suggestion, why not wait in the hall?
We've made ourselves scarce now, so we'll shout April Fool!

Marilyn M Fowler

APRIL 1ST

We really got you going!
Ha! I saw the anger in your eyes
Never seen so much to despise
Made me feel kind of special.
Sorry it's turned out this way
We lost the tracks and broke the rules
Hey, it's only an April Fools
I'm sorry I slept with your best mate!
For goodness sake!
We really got you going
Ha! The smell really freaked you out
Oh, and the way you stammered about
Made me feel only slightly guilty.
Sorry it's turned out this way.
We lost the tracks and broke the rules
Did I tell you it's just April Fools,
I'm sorry we microwaved your cat!
Yeah well, we also burnt down your flat
I don't see why you're taking it so bad
I mean, we didn't know it was your dad
Who owned the car with no brakes
For goodness sakes!
Relax, it's just your mum floating in the pool
Hey! It's just April Fools.
I said I was sorry about the glass
Who would have known how sharp it could get
Hey, don't get so upset
There's nothing I can say
Except, who needs fingers anyway?
And I'm sorry I cut up your clothes
And for the punch in the nose
It's just the way we went a little crazy
I'm sorry, is everything a little hazy?

That'll be the poison in your tea
Bet you didn't guess it was me
Who lost the tracks and broke the rules
Don't be so serious
It's just April Fools.

Claire Farragher

APRIL FOOL

When my brother was twelve years old
And I was four years younger,
He said my pants were falling down -
In horror I looked down to see-
'April Fool' he called after me.

Phyllis M Dunn

APRIL FOOL

When playing basketball at school
I had a rest and sat upon a stool
Then the teacher came to ask
'Will you do me a special task?
Go to the janitor I demand
Then you must ask for a long stand'
So stand I did for quite a while
The floor was hard its covering tile
Getting angry, losing my cool
My teacher shouts 'April Fool.'

C Halliburton

The Know-All

The small girl stood at my side
Tell me, she said
Why do birds take to flight?
Why does the moon shine by night?
Why do I play?
Why do I have to go to school?
And say my prayers at night?
Why does my doggy drool?
Why do I sometimes cry?
What is the rainbow made of?
And, why do we hate flies?

Well! I said to the little darling
Do you think I am a sage
With a long white beard
And hair worn unbecoming
I would need to be one
To answer one of your age.

Oh no! Ma'am she retorted
I don't ask for fancy tricks
But at the shop up the street
The ladies said when you were passing
'Anything you want to know
She'll never keep you guessing.'

'Well!' said I. Quite surprised
'Did they also tell you my name?'
'Yes Ma'am' said the little darling
Her pretty face earnest and wise
They said 'Mrs Know-all is just passing'
I followed you Ma'am, please answer my 'Whys'.

Marguerite Porthouse

HAIR (A PERSONAL REFLECTION)

Hair no longer grows on my head.
It grows in my ears instead, and it
flows in locks across my shoulders.
My back looks more like a horse
as the galloping years make me older.

Hair won't grow on my head anymore
but it wildly sprouts from my nostrils,
that's for sure.
I can't say I like it, not one bit,
but despite this confusing profusion
and alarming relocation,
this hirsute revelation,
there is one thing now I realise,
one thing I could never hate.
It's that cultured gleam
from my polished pate.

Peter Bauer

LARA'S LAW

You've heard of old Sod's Law, of course -
It's famous far and wide -
How any falling piece of bread
Lands on its buttered side.

But there is something far more dire,
Its outcome very sure:
A trick my little cat thought up
That's known as Lara's Law.

Don't sit with muesli on your lap
When Lara is around,
For though you thought her fast asleep
She'll be there in one bound!

In kitten days she'd land in soup
(But quickly found it burned),
So then she'd knock it to the ground
(But had her efforts spurned).

So now she jumps with agile grace
Upon my breakfast tray,
Then quickly off again, to raise
A cloud of milky spray.

Her party piece (if luck holds good)
Is on and off, between
The cereal and the drinking mug -
One must not make a scene,

Or down will come the coffee cup
The sugar bowl will fall,
While Lara rushing from the mess,
Treads wheatgerm down the hall.

So in our house, don't ask for more
You might get caught by Lara's Law.

Jackie Durnin

HEARTSOB

It happened so fast I couldn't take stock
Decree nisi papers came as such a shock
Should I celebrate of should I go moody
At being divorced from my beloved Trudy?

At first I must confess there was a sense of relief
At being freed from her nagging DIY grief
But I thought of her bod and her wondrous home cooking
Quite often her as Delia Smith men were always mistooking.

At mentioning her name my knees do go a'quiver
For Delia makes my very bone marrow shiver
Her delicious way of holding the wok and saucepan
Captivates me in a way no other woman can.

Trudy teased me about my obsession for Delia:
'It's not me you want, it's the meal, yah?'
I blushed scarlet and denied the truth a lot
But Trudy knew and of me she wanted shot.

Now I'm alone and fending solely for one
It's so peaceful though with Trudy gone
I can watch football in peace and leave the washing 'til morn
And a huge poster of Delia in my bedroom can now adorn.

N C Bain

Anno Domini

After the age of sixty-five
We're lucky enough to survive;
But then our troubles really start,
And slowly then we fall apart.

In youth our strength was our great pride
As needed in a rugger side;
But then the muscle starts to shrink,
It's far from fair we surely think.

Then frustration sets in too,
At all the things we cannot do;
That long ago we did with ease,
And with a deftness sure to please.

In our seventies sight grows dim
And hearing too becomes quite grim.
Joints grow stiff and fingers quiver,
While cold weather makes us shiver.

Oh! What then will our eighties bring?
They will not make us dance and sing.
In point of fact it will get worse,
And shortly we will need a nurse!

Thus it is - so goes the rumour -
Thank God for my sense of humour,
So I can say quite cheerfully
I'm wearing out quite gracefully.

A O Jones

JOY OF FRIENDSHIP

What I like to say about is true friendship, good laughter and joy.
We have always been honest and open with each other
So I have to be completely open now
And let you know about our wonderful friendship.
A shoulder to cry on, good to talk to each other, good laughter!
Our true friendship.
So happy to have a good friend.
The joy of friendship will stay until the end of time.

P Patel

Laughter - The Best Medicine

On a day trip to Cleethorpes,
An old lady friend and I went
Full of pip and excitement
Until our bus pulled up
At our destination, 'Oh heck'

Everybody was heard to say
As the rain just pelted down,
Oh what a blooming morning
Out of the bus we all trooped,
Umbrellas, macs all ready for the day.

'Well, luv' I said to my friend
'We'll go for a nice cup of tea,
Then take a walk along the front.'
We did just that then this is
What we heard 'Ho ho, hee hee'

My friend and I joined in
With 'Ho ho' and 'Hee hee'
Doubled up with laughter
Come join in - spread it
Around your office, it is free.
Laughter, medicine for all
So 'Ho ho' and 'Hee hee.'

We were ready for home
After day well spent,
Oh here we go again 'Ho ho, hee hee'
Not such a bad day at all
For a copper or two out,
Of figure of a bobby, we
received laughter, best medicine
For all, so altogether 'Ho ho, hee hee.'

Kathleen Willis

THE ELEPHANT

'By 'eck,' remarked the elephant, 'it's a funny do an' all,
That I'm stuck 'ere inside this zoo wi' nowt to do at all.
I should be wanderin' the plains, a'wavin' of me tusks
At passin' buck and wildebeest, not stood 'ere eatin' rusks
And stuff that babies chuck at me from buggies by me pen!
(I allus toss 'em out. but they just chuck. 'em in again)
And as for what I'm given in the way of daily rations,
I'm sure it's got some additives to dampen down me passions!
There's clearly nowt for me in 'ere, I think I'll do a bunk.
The fence will be a doddle if I rock it with me trunk!
I can deftly stamp it down a bit, try not to make a row.
Then I'll wander round the zoo a while to make me final bow.
Away I'll trot, across the moor, beneath the scuddin' cloud.
And when she hears what I have done, me Mam'll be real proud!
I'll trample all the farmers' fields and gobble up the wheat,
And root up lots of trees and such. Eeh! Life'll be a treat!
So when you read the headlines or hear it on TV,
New sighting of huge, savage beast
It'll just be little me!'

Jean Oxley

OUR BABY LIAM

When you laugh
We feel rich
In love.
In a hard world,
We worry so much
About money.
All of our children
Money could never compare
To the joy they bring.
We should not worry.
We will always
Laugh with you.

__Lee Round__

HAIKU MUSINGS AT THE ZOO

the white tiger yawned
you're no longer my hero
thought the little girl

two lambs stared at her
believing she was a wolf
'what big fangs you have!'

a toad croaked unseen
'they think this is Noah's ark
but there's still no flood'

what has a long neck
stinks to high heaven and has
lovely eyelashes?

'yo' said the raven
'yeah' echoed the kangaroo
'shush' whistled the snake

where's Tommy the chimp?
snoozing behind Rip the Mule
dreaming bananas

they gave each other
the once over, beast and man
asking who was who

a pretty woman
vowed to seduce a baboon
but he ignored her

then God changed his mind
ordering the gates open
all humans were banned

Albert Russo

RAISE THE TONE

I went base over apex
Carrying a dozen eggs and flour
The family laughed
Thought it a hoot and howl.

I sat and cried
Nursing my pride
Oh what a waste
I could have died.

What's that laugh with
Weep alone
Bruised landing gear
Colours will soon tone.

Give me the bucket
I'll soon kick that
Who'll have the last laugh
When I buy a new hat?

Ann Weavers

LAUGHTER

Laugh and the world laughs with you
Is a saying old but true
But people laugh in different ways
Hearty ones that strain their stays
Others titter and hold it in
While some laugh out loud and make a din
Laughter shared such happy times
Appreciated like some old wines
A happy face makes you smile
And life feels good just for a while
Children enjoying life, laughter flows free
A good example for you and me
So when you feel down and rather sad
Think of something that makes you glad
Then you can feel laughter bubbling up inside
Let it take over like the rushing tide
For laughter makes the world go round
And costs you nothing, this joyful sound.

Norah M Bennett

TRANSFORMATION
(Dedicated to my son Michael George Milne)

I long for fields of hazy lemon glow
To hear the crystal waters, meandering below
A swallow's glide, on effervescent air
Listening to the willow trees, dancing, debonair
Let a thousand shades of colour fill my eye
An animated cotton cloud in a perfect azure sky
So take me from this chrysalis, unfold my wings again
And bring me back the warm spring sun
To dry away my rain.

N A Milne

LIFE GROWS LIKE THAT

I was told as a little girl,
Like flowers, baby girls bloomed like seeds.
I remember thinking after that,
Are baby boys then the weeds?

Debra Neale

LAUGHTER

Now once, with others comes the time
To contrive by circumstance with mischievous eyes
Inflating a story, adjusting the lines, as
Their interest grows their smiles will arise.

This is the beginning of laughter time
You hold them, acting the story so real, they
Believe for that moment, as the gestures play down
The actual person you really are.

Becoming an actor upon a stage, your gift of
Expression is not prelaid. You speak from your
Soul, you are giving to others.
The relief they desire and the laughter will follow.

The sharing you have given in the act you have played
Will return a million times or more.
The laughter an echo, from some distant shore,
Laps continual sounds as a pebble once thrown
In an endless pool creating waves unknown.

Such is your joy through the pain you have shared.

John G Horley

GENE CRAZY

I had a terrible nightmare I ate
Genetic foods
They took a gene from an earthworm
And put it in my booze
Now when I get all tiddly on the
Floor I go all wriggly
Why did they put that gene inside
my booze?

Now they are putting genes
everything
This will be our fate
When you sit down to your dinner
There will be more genes on your plate

When they create these nasty genes in
There's no way of putting them back
So if they take a gene from a piece of coal
It could make us all go black

What a terrible thing if this came
true
A gene from a washing powder could turn us blue
A gene from a snake could make you
shake
From my nightmare from my bed I wake.

Bert Booley

SHIRLEY'S 50TH

Well old girl, the day has come
You're fifty now, it's not much fun.
There's really nothing to shout about
Your teeth will probably all fall out.
Rheumatism, gout, arthritis and more
You're really going to feel very sore
I'd give up now if I were you
Don't just sit there going boo-hoo.
Old age beckons, it's saying 'Come here -
I've got some surprises for you, my dear.
I'll take all your faculties, you'll be well rid
Just get in the dustbin and bang down the lid.
And if you start to rant and moan
They might try and put you in a home.'
Yes, it all looks bleak, it's very true
There's really nothing you can do.
But never mind, you're not alone
There's always somebody at the end of the 'phone.
Whenever you're in any doubt
Just give me a ring - I'll sort you out!

Carol Somerfield

THE HOSPITAL VISIT

It took me twenty minutes to find a parking place,
Then six flights of stairs to get to you, my dear.
The alternative was the box they call the lift.
You had to be a sprinter to get in and out of this.

At last, I arrive on your floor.
I pat my hair, brush my dress,
Put on this great big stupid grin,
Then push my way through the swing doors, let the visit begin.

I look around for you in all the beds,
But can't find you anywhere.
Just strange eyes looking up at me,
I smile at them, no response, just a vacant stare.

In a small side ward I see you laying on the bed.
Not pale and forlorn and suffering as I had thought,
But bright-eyed laying there like Cleopatra
Surrounded by flowers, succulent fruit and smiling from ear to ear.

I stayed with you for an hour or two.
Enjoying the talk of doctors and medical things.
Then it's goodbye, see you soon, I feel on top of the world
But oh dear, you do look a bit pale, have I overdone this visiting?

Dawn Shaw

THE DIVINE CHUCKLE

When God designed the camel, chimp, giraffe and kangaroo,
the walrus with its whiskers, the pelicans with beaks;
when he beheld the elephant, the hippo and gnu,
I wonder if he chuckled at his own created freaks?

A brilliant thought occurred to him in his vast cosmic plan
He needed some amusement in his universe, alone
He'd make a human being in his image, call him 'man'
Give him a body, mind, freewill, and add - a funny bone!

And down the centuries man has used his humour and his wit
to ridicule hypocrisy and pierce inflated pride
God's gift has been a blessing to the clown and satirist
and politicians have to take derision in their stride!

The smiling mask of courage often hides man's fear and pain
The therapy of cheerfulness is rarely known to fail
To see the funny side of things can so relax the strain
Did Jonah give a belly laugh when wedged inside the whale?

Margaret Holmes

Teething Troubles

To look smart for our recent 'Golden Wedding' luncheon, a dental plate my husband had,
Because his family all badgered him with saying 'Dad, that gap does look bad!'

So, to the dentist, under protest, he did go, and the necessary wire plate was made.
All went well, and so on our surprise 'Golden Wedding' holiday to the USA we did go,
But for reasons best known to Dad, he was adamant that those dentures in, to eat, he could not abide!
So tactfully he removed them, and in his pocket did hide!

Returning home from our trip, no teeth could be found,
In spite of searching every possible place, upstairs and down.
It seems the missing dentures were causing us more than just a frown!

Two days later, cutting the back lawns, hubby thought 'That's a big stone to go through my mowing machine!
Yes! you've guessed it, the two wired teeth, in a bumpy ride had been!

Recovering from frustration and shock, and then, of course, sheer delight at finding those 'falsies' had been lying in the grass, all night!
This has caused a laugh for family and friends, as this funny episode we recall,
Little do we know what unexpected mishaps on us, can befall.

Just a postscript to this tale of woe,
Those dentures have finally decided to go!
'Cause hubby dropped them out of his pocket, in the garden - yet again
But this time he stood on them - all bent - no more good
Oh! what a crying shame.

So the 'gap' remains, comments are made and those dentures remain wrapped up in a drawer,
Must be for sentimental memories, hubby is keeping them for!

J Greenacre

FISHING IN THE STREET

Fishing in the street I went,
crazy though that sounds,
not as balmy as you think,
a cod or two I caught.

Gerald helped me land the fish,
a plastic bag was used,
I wasn't sure what he did mean,
'You've killed it now' he said.

I banged the cod upon his head,
extinguished all his life,
it didn't really dawn on me,
I'd killed a part of me.

The moral of this story,
is plain as plain can be,
when killing off another's soul,
a part of you will die.

So when you have the chance to save,
a fish, a frog, or toad,
just remember if you can,
it's you, you could be saving.

Paul Wadge

SMILE

Lighten up your feelings
See the happy side
Smiling thro' your troubles
Sadder feelings hide

If you smile at someone
You get your smile returned
That should tell you something
A lesson to be learned

We all love the good times
Happy, bright and gay
Keep your jolly humour
And troubles fade away

Sheila M Gannon

LAUGHING AT YOU

I could not stop laughing at you
You were so funny last night
All dressed up in that old gear
Trying so hard to make us catch fright.

I could not stop laughing at you
As you went to bed
For you had got everything just mixed up
Waving that old sword around your head.

I could not stop laughing at you
The more upset you got
For you said that it was not you as we woke you up
For you say you have been asleep all evening
Just rocking in your cot.

Keith L Powell

THE HAIRCUT

The foreman looked round the factory floor
But his young apprentice lad was not there
As time passed by, the foreman's anger burned
And exploded as the lad returned
'Where have you been? Don't give me no ifs or buts'
'Why gaffer, I've been to have my hair cut'
'What, in the firm's time?'
'Well it grows in the firm's time, doesn't it?'
'Not all of it grows, so don't you scoff'
'That's why I didn't get it all cut off!'

Gordon Bannister

Catalyst!

It was a very solemn congregation,
Until a baby's chuckle broke surrounding ice.
Spreading as a sudden conflagration,
Transforming and thawing in a trice.
Eye contact with nearest neighbour,
Nods and smiles with softening face,
Realising laughter is not *such* a labour,
Happiness can be a saving grace.
A giggle like a ripple stirred the crowd,
Heaving ribs broke dams in their throats,
And then at last one dares to laugh aloud,
Wiped tears and others' shoulders smote.
Innocent small catalyst to enjoyment,
Joined in the widening movement it began,
And laughter surely is the best employment,
For vocal chords of both a babe and man!

Di Bagshawe

LITTLE GREEN-EYED GOD

The furtive glance, the eyes that meet
So fleetingly, but tell it all.
How can I bear the thought of her,
And he, my man, with twinkling eyes.
Oh, little green eyed god. Beware.
Dumpy body, simpering smile.
Legs, like piano, short and plump.
What can he see in her? While I,
So elegant and tall and fair.
With sylphlike body, shapely legs.
I've passed my prime, I must admit,
But so has she, so what is it?
Oh, little green-eyed god. Beware.
Now here he comes that man of mine
With roving eyes and stealthy hands,
As round my waist his arms entwine.

Monica F James

RED RIDIN' RAP

Now this here's the tale about 'Ridin' Hood'
    Who went for a walk in the big bad wood
A-singin' an' a-skippin' without any care
    Of the big bad wolf she was . . . unaware . . .

Red was off to Gran's on one of her trips
    Unaware o' Wolfie a-lickin' his lips
He was anticipatin' how Red would be
    In a lip-smackin', mouth-waterin' . . . fricassee . . .

A little time a-now into little Red's chore
    We find her a-knockin' at Grandma's door

'Come in - come in Red my dear . . . Nanna's here; so have no fear'

Red is in and Grandma grins . . . an' now the horror bit begins

'Oh Grannie, Grannie! What big eyes'
('Oh no! Has she sussed thro' my disguise?')

'All the better to see yuh kid! Now what's in the basket?
Open the lid.'

'Oh Grannie! What big ears you've got'
('This kid sure susses things a lot')

All the better to hear yuh speak; now kiss your Nanna on her dainty cheek.'

'Oh Grannie! What big shiny teeth'

'Spare us kid! Us wolves gotta eat.'

Now 'Gran' leapt up with alacrity
But Red saw red an' she used her knee
You see! She'd sussed through Bad's disguise
An' she said . . . 'You fool! It was the eyes . . .
    . . . an' beside you bein' a different sex . . .
    . . . didn't you know my Nan wore specs?'

As she pinned poor Wolfie to the cabin floor
      Red's woodcutter daddy came a-through the door
As woodcutters would he was totin' an axe
      With which he gave ol' 'Bad' a coupla whacks
  'Are you okay daughter?' he said to Red
      A-pullin' Grannie from under the bed
As she put in her teeth - she stomped her feet
Then she screamed at Red . . . *'When do we eat?'*

. . . Now the moral of this simple tale; is a recipe that'll never fail
If you ever go a-walkin' in a lonely wood - don't ever cross forks with
. . . *Ridin' Hood!*

Norm Whittle

DIAMOND WEDDING

'It's been a long time,
A long, long time . . .' said she,
'Aah umm, ah! It has . . . indeed
It has . . .' said he;
'And gone by quick enough, you know,
So quick . . . it seems to me . . .'
'It has at that . . . ah! Yes, you're right,
It has at that . . .' said he.

'But we've been happy enough
With ups and downs . . . and
Through it all . . .' said she;
'Aah! Yes, happy, yes . . . we've been
Happy . . . me and thee . . .'

'*You* haven't changed . . . not an awful lot,
Not much that I can see . . .'
'Aah umm . . . eh? Well, well,
You don't think so?' said he;
'Oh! What I mean . . . you umm and aah!
And always you'd agree!'
'Well aah! old gal . . . it's paid me too . . .
Well . . . aah! Ha ha!'
Said he.

R Gaveston-Knight

GIRDS

When I was just a girl, I was very fond of girds;
If you're not sure just what I mean, I'll put it into words,
They didn't cost a penny-piece, we found them on the shore,
Old rims from wheels of bicycles that washed up near our door.

I bowled my gird along the road with wallops from a stick,
And guided it to right and left with casual expert flick;
But, still my great ambition, which no rusty bike rim matched,
Was to possess a metal hoop, with ring and rod attached.

One day I did get hold of one that hung upon a wall,
So keen was I to try it out, I felt quite ten feet tall;
Until I had my first attempt - and couldn't make it go!
To find it wasn't easy, was an unexpected blow.

A hundred times I tried that hoop and couldn't keep it straight,
It wobbled here, and wobbled there, with crazy stumbling gait;
Then, one more try, this time it worked, and ran just like a dream,
Along the road we sped in style, a smoothly balanced team.

I kept on going like the wind, as fast as I could run,
With iron hoop beside me, singing loudly as it spun;
I whooped with sheer excitement, I was happy as could be,
And then, I tripped upon a stone, and fell and skinned my knee!

Janet Brown

The Appointment Card

Sitting sweating, swallow hard, it says toothhearty (2.30)
on my appointment card.

This time really is a rotten pun I can feel the tingle in my gum
a sickly sound from the other room drilling, filling
I hope this injection is really pain-killing.

My name is called and time stands still,
the dentist knows he's a tooth to fill.

He stands there smiling all gleaming gnashers,
I don't want this torture I'd rather have the forty lashes.

Shaun Gilberton

LAUGHTER, THE BEST MEDICINE

Like a babbling brook, a chuckle starts
A river of sound that swells and flows.
It brings tears to the eye and a face that glows.
Each laugh so different, so special to hear.
It moves and spreads, infecting all who are near.
Driving away depression, anxiety, fear and pain,
Making life worth living again.
Presses right through until sudden release.
Inhibitions and fears all just have to cease.
It brings health to the body, healing to the soul.
Joy to the hearer, filling the deepest of holes.
There is nothing quite like it, merriment and mirth.
Let it grow large inside you and then give it birth.

Barbara Gates

THE TOO-BIG-YIN

See, *ah* was too fat, N'at
A'roond where ah sat, N'at
So, doc gie'd me a diet, N'at
Jist for tae try it, N'at
He said, eat plent fruit, N'at
An' ye might fit yer suit, N'at
So, ah took his advice, N'at
Nae matter the price, N'at
Yet the price o' some fruits, N'at
Could've got me *two* suits, N'at
Ah ate apple rings, N'at
An' prunes an' fig things, N'at
Stopped eatin' bics, N'at
Did aerobics for kicks, N'at
Guzzled yin-calory coke, N'at
That gie'd ye the boak, N'at
But the upshot o' that, N'at
Was, ah put on *mair* fat, N'at!"
N'en the trouble-n-strife, N'at
Mah beloved, the wife, N'at
Gie'd me second advice, N'at
Which she roared in a trice, N'at
She said, you'll only shrink, N'at
When ye gie up the *drink,* N'at!

Bob Mackay

LO, THE POOR FARMER

The tractor exploded midst whistles and farts,
'It's so bloody old that you can't get the parts,'
Thus moaned the farmer, just cursing his fate,
'How can a man make a profit old mate.
The rains in July, have flattened my corn,
Sometimes I wish I had never been born.
Someone has poisoned my whole flock of goats,
And my wife's up at Selfridges buying fur coats.'
His tales of bad luck would bring tears to your eyes,
He'll live on his losses until his demise.
This farmer is now a great man to be feared,
His tumbledown farmhouse has long disappeared.
A million-pound mansion now stands in its place,
But he still has that woebegone look on his face.
He is almost in tears as he takes off his coat,
Asks the barmaid to change him a hundred-pound note.
He will take out his friends in his Mercedes Benz
And you may all scoff if you like!
He will tell you he's poor as he goes out the door,
But you'll never see him on a bike!

Norman Chandler

Pavonia

Lady of love,
embrace me with your trident stare,
passion abiding midnight eyes,
dark pearls that speak to me of care,
your essence, my first wishful heavenly prayer

Angelic is your caressive presence,
hurried is my poetic yearning,
calm is your seduction,
my wide eyes and poetic pen faithfully learning

Poetry embraces me

Pavonia, Roman goddess,
her unveiling tresses of midnight blesses,
command me to your elegance,
heavenly temptress

My untouched soul,
receives your kiss,
grant my prayers true,
so I may call to the unfortunate few,
that dwell from my present view

Burn my heart with joy,
tempt me no longer,
my pen has writ of your wonder,
Pavonia, slave to my yearning,
I be the slave of beauty conjuring,
from the burning passion of your skin,
with every desire I long to be your king

Pavonia, queen of purest feature,
you are a poets most favoured teacher,
my simply beautiful creature

Paul Cozens

THE LAST LAUGH

The old girl lay a-dying,
Her folks stood round her bed.
She called her grandson to her,
And this is what she said.

'Just now you have some missing teeth,
But in a little while,
The new ones will be good to see,
So don't forget to smile.'

'And let your joyous laugh ring out,
And misery will depart,
For laughter is the biggest cure,
To ease a broken heart.'

The little lady softly said
'For me, my dears, don't weep,'
And on her face a sweet smile spread,
She turned and went to sleep.

In this case laughter couldn't cure,
But final thoughts she had,
That laughter was a healing gift.
That surely can't be bad.

Margaret Thorpe

THE CHARMED LIFE OF FINNY THE FISH

Spare a thought for a fish
   his mind is being abused
he needs some attention
   the poor chap is really confused

Finny the fish is so brave
   he cannot resist the bait
alas, as he nibbles at it
   he is aware of his fate

So, as usual, he's hooked
   he sees his maker in the flesh
he thinks he's breathed his last
   as he is absolutely fresh

The human hooks it over
   unhooks this possible meal
then returns it to the water
   confused? How would you feel?

The fish is really delighted
   he has had a lucky escape
he felt somewhat dejected
   as he swam with mouth agape

He really felt quite lucky
   he'll be out for a meal next time
once more, he was tossed back
   what, he wondered was his crime

Trevor Vincent

SUBMISSIONS INVITED
SOMETHING FOR EVERYONE

POETRY NOW '99 - Any subject, any style, any time.

WOMENSWORDS '99 - Strictly women, have your say the female way!

STRONGWORDS '99 - Warning! Age restriction, must be between 16-24, opinionated and have strong views. (Not for the faint-hearted)

All poems no longer than 30 lines.
Always welcome! No fee!
Cash Prizes to be won!

Mark your envelope (eg *Poetry Now*) **'99**
Send to:
Forward Press Ltd
Remus House, Coltsfoot Drive,
Woodston,
Peterborough, PE2 9JX

OVER £10,000 POETRY PRIZES TO BE WON!

Judging will take place in October 1999